92% of dinner is what to make

DOES THIS SOUND FAMILIAR?

- Sick of making time-consuming family dinners every night, and need a break now and then?
- Living alone and don't always want the hassle of fancy cooking for one?
- Can't cook, not really interested in learning, but happy to spend a short while making something simple?
- Don't want to rely overly on high-salt, high-fat and high-sugar pre-packaged meals from the supermarket?
- Finding regular takeaway too expensive?
- Tried other cookbooks that promise quick and easy meals; but still having trouble finding quick, easy meals?
- Happy to eat food that's somewhere between edible and gourmet?

This cookbook doesn't pretend to be a proper cookbook: you won't find beautifully plated national television-worthy style meals, but nor will you be opening two cans and mixing them together, calling that "cooking". Instead, you'll find some food hacks that work for singles and families, that you can use with limited ingredients. In lots of the meals there are options for substitutions to mix things up a little, so lunches and dinners don't get too stale. Some of these ideas contain only two ingredients, but when you add them together with another simple recipe it's good enough for a meal.

FOOD HACKS

COOKBOOK

FOR BUSY PEOPLE

WITH GENUINELY EASY AND PASSABLY HEALTHY

FOOD TO COOK, MAKE OR ASSEMBLE WHEN YOU CAN'T BE BOTHERED

Copyright © 2024 by Nicole Taylor

All rights reserved.

No portion of this book may be reproduced in any form without written permission from the publisher or author, except as permitted by Australian copyright law.

Published by IngramSpark

ISBN 978-0-6488642-3-3

I've also found some great products in the supermarket you may not have tried before.

Recipe Ratings	
*	Too easy; may contain some boiling or frying, then just add together
**	Still easy, with some chopping or quick cooking involved.
***	Easy, but with a bit more cooking and a few more ingredients. Should still take you less than 30 minutes.

Notes

- Wash all raw vegetables carefully.
- There is no need to peel potato skins, they are edible and nutritious.
- Other root vegetables sometimes need to be peeled if the skin is dirty or a little old. Younger vegetables do not need to be peeled, e.g. baby carrots.
- Let's mention seasoning…. I try not to season anything with salt, even plain vegetables. I've been able to get used to unsalted food with a bit of practice, but if you feel the need to add salt to any recipe then go for it.

CONTENTS

COUSCOUS 11
    Couscous with Egg 12
POLENTA 13
    Basic Polenta 13
    Fried Polenta 14
RICE 14
    Rice Pilaf 15
    Rice with a Boiled Egg 16
VEGETABLES 18
    Raw Vegetable Salad 19
    Bruschetta 21
    Baked Cauliflower 22
    Baked Creamy Cauliflower 23
    Brussel Sprouts 24
    Miso Eggplant 25
    Zucchini and Haloumi Stack 27
    Caramelised Onion 27
    Corn and Cottage Cheese 28
    Corn Fritters 28
    Mashed Potato 29

Roast Potato, Sweet Potato, Pumpkin, Onion 30
Creamed Spinach 31
Noodles with Vegetables 32
EGGS 34
Omelette 34
TOFU 37
Sesame Soy Tofu 37
Peanut Tofu 39
CHICKEN 42
Precooked Chicken 42
Honey Soy Chicken 43
SOUPS 45
Chicken Soup 45
Pea and Ham Soup 47
Chicken and Corn Soup 48
MEATBALLS 49
Meatballs 49
Meatball in a Roll 51
PRE-MADE SUPERMARKET MEALS 53
Marinated Steaks in Vacuum Sealed Packs 53
Fresh Fish 54
Frozen Fish, Scallops or Prawns 55
Lemon Butter Sauce 55

Dumplings (Yum Cha style) 55
Hot Smoked Salmon in Vacuum Sealed Packs 57
Burritos and Tacos 58
PASTA 60
Creamy Pasta with Greens 60
PUFF PASTRY PIZZA 63
CURRIES 64
DELI DINNERS 66
SANDWICHES 69
Sandwich Suggestions 69
Club Sandwich 70
SAUCES 73
Salad Dressing with Miso 73
Peanut Dressing for Meat or Tofu 73
Sauce for Fish 74
DESSERTS 75
French Toast 75
Tapioca 76
Bread and Butter Pudding 77
Custard 78
Polenta Porridge 79
INDEX 82
REFERENCES 84

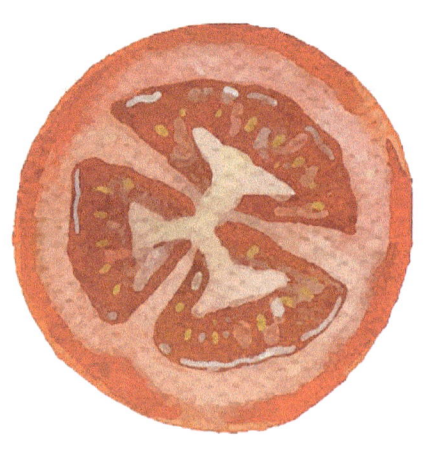

COUSCOUS
*

Couscous is a wonderful "filler" food – it goes with almost anything, is healthy and can be prepared in about 10 minutes with minimal intervention. Look for Israeli couscous, which has a large sized grain and comes in different flavours (my favourite is the wholewheat). Because it's a dried food you can stash it in your cupboard for ages; look for it in the health food aisle, health food shops or online.

All brands are slightly different, so follow the instructions on the pack, but once you're used to it you can do what I do: boil about 250-300ml of stock or water in a small saucepan, add enough couscous until there is about 1cm of liquid to cover the couscous, and simmer until all the liquid is absorbed. Then just turn off the heat, cover it, and leave for at least 7 minutes; it will stay hot for a while. *(Note: Do read the instructions first. Some types of couscous will need more liquid and therefore will need longer to simmer).*

When you're about to eat, add a knob of butter or other butter substitute spread, stir it gently through and dish it up. This amount will make a good-sized helping for 2 people as an addition to another recipe (or just eat it alone from a bowl… nothing wrong about that).

Use couscous as a substitute for rice - it's quicker to cook - or pasta - it's healthier.

Couscous with Egg
*

The ultimate in quick food preparation: simply prepare your couscous, serve into a bowl and place a warm soft-boiled egg on top. The combination is perfect – your children may even like it. We often have this as a snack in between meals.

Tip: I use an egg cooker to make perfect boiled eggs every time, see page 68.

POLENTA

Like couscous, polenta can be prepared in minutes and is a great filler, even for desserts. It should be made so that it is just slightly wet: not runny, but not stodgy. You can refrigerate leftovers and reheat quickly on the stove by adding a bit of water or milk and stirring. I use polenta as a substitute for pasta, couscous or rice for any dish.

Basic Polenta
*

- Polenta, 50g
- Stock, about 200ml
- Butter or butter substitute, 20g
- Grated parmesan or other cheese, 30g (optional)

Boil the stock, then add the polenta while stirring. It will thicken quickly. Keep stirring until it is creamy (about 5 minutes). If it looks too lumpy or dry, add a little water. Add butter and cheese, continue stirring until mixed through. Leave for a few minutes with the lid on, then serve.

This will make two helpings to be served with something else, or you can just eat it by itself. Leftovers can be reheated the next day with a little water.

Fried Polenta
**

Use the polenta recipe from above, but instead of eating it right away, spread it in a tray and put it in the fridge. When you want to cook it, cut it into squares (it will have set firm) and lightly fry or grill in a little butter or oil.

RICE

White rice is quick, but brown rice is better for you if you have the time.

- For brown rice, it cooks more quickly if you can soak it first – 2 hours or overnight in an amount of lukewarm water 2 or 3 times the amount of rice. Drain and rinse, cover with lots of hot water and boil gently until soft. For soaked rice, about 20 minutes; for dry rice, about 30. Drain, then put back into the same saucepan, covered, off the heat, for 10 minutes. A cup of rice makes about 2 cooked cups.
- For white rice, add 2 cups of water to every 1 cup of rice, simmer for 15 to 20 minutes with the lid on and check to see when water is absorbed (don't stir, this will make it mushy). When the liquid is all absorbed and the rice is soft to taste, leave in the pan, covered, off the heat for about 10 minutes. This will make 2 cups of rice.

Try Rice Pilaf. This is a simple way to cook white long grain rice and is a real treat.

Rice Pilaf
**

- 1 small Onion, finely chopped
- 200g White long grain rice
- 300 ml Stock or water, enough to cover rice
- Tablespoon of butter or butter substitute
- Saucepan with a metal handle that can be used in the oven

Preheat oven to 180 degrees for about 15 minutes (it is important to do this. You will know how long your food has been cooking at the right temperature).

Warm half of the butter in the saucepan. Add chopped onion and cook gently for about 5 minutes to soften, but not brown the onion. Add the rice and stir, cooking gently for about another 5 minutes.

Add the stock, which should be hot if possible (if it isn't, it will take longer to boil). The stock should cover the rice with one centimetre of liquid over the top of the rice. Add a little water if necessary. Bring to the boil.

Put the lid on the saucepan and place in the oven for 18 minutes. Take it out (make sure you use oven gloves!) and rest on the top of the stove for another 15 minutes, with the lid on.

Stir through the rest of the butter and serve.

Rice with a Boiled Egg
**

Just like couscous with a boiled egg, you can have a bowl of rice with a soft-boiled egg mixed through for a quick meal that's reasonably filling.

If you have more time, try mixing through some vegetables, which you can either quickly pan fry or microwave to soften. Some examples:

- Carrot, grated
- Corn, tinned or fresh
- Broccoli or broccolini, chopped, and don't waste the stumps; they are edible
- Mushroom, chopped/sliced (pan fry, do not microwave)
- Zucchini, chopped/sliced
- Baby corn, tinned or fresh, whole pieces are fine
- Yellow squash, chopped

Try pan frying in sesame oil, peanut oil or other for a different flavour.

VEGETABLES

We all know they're good for you, but it's often hard to get enough in our diet. I'd be lying if I said I ate my recommended five cups every day.

If I'm really feeling lazy, I'll just steam a few different vegetables in a saucepan steamer – corn cobs, broccoli, green beans, snow peas, baby Brussels sprouts and peas are some favourites – and eat them plain with some protein like fish, meat or egg. Steaming vegetables is my favourite way to cook them – it is unbelievably quick (most vegetables will cook in just a few minutes, if you like them semi-crunchy), easy to test for readiness and keeps much of the nutrition.

Don't be afraid to use frozen vegetables! They are said to contain more vitamins than fresh ones. They are cheap and because they can be stored for months, you can always have them on hand. Try frozen peas, cauliflower, broccoli and beans. - and especially edamame, available frozen and already out of their pods if you're not interested in shelling (I'm not).

Raw Vegetable Salad
**

Roughly chop or slice any of the following (about 1cm pieces):

- Green beans
- Broccoli
- Cauliflower
- Capsicum (red or yellow are sweetest)
- Carrot
- Zucchini

- Purple cabbage
- Brussels sprouts
- Celery
- Fennel
- Cauliflower
- Apple (*this is highly recommended; I use it in every salad. It will sweeten the other ingredients perfectly.*)

No need to chop these:

- Baby corn, fresh or tinned
- Baby tomatoes
- Edamame beans
- Sprouts, any kind of fresh ones
- Other tinned beans, rinsed thoroughly, well drained: cannellini, red beans, borlotti, four bean mixes

To make this salad even more tasty and fulfilling, add one or more of these:

- Danish or other feta
- Haloumi, after lightly frying some slices to char it
- Water chestnuts, tinned and strained
- Chopped nuts – almonds, walnuts, pine nuts, etc.
- Hard boiled eggs, sliced

- Tin of lentils, strained

You will note that **all** the fresh ingredients are crunchy ones. I don't usually make salads with leafy greens or cut tomatoes because they go soggy too quickly. With this salad, if there's any left over, it will last a day or two.

For dressing, you can simply use a few spoons of olive oil – make sure the apples are well covered, and a few generous splashes of balsamic vinegar. Squeeze a lemon in as well, if you have one handy. Or, use any other dressing you have handy.

Bruschetta
**

If you can make the topping an hour or two in advance, the onion will be sweeter as it absorbs the dressing.

Portions of ingredients will make one serve.

- ❖ Bread, thickly sliced if possible, 2 pieces
- ❖ Tomatoes, 2 large
- ❖ Red onion, about ¼
- ❖ Olive oil, a splash

- ❖ Lemon juice, about a teaspoon
- ❖ Balsamic vinegar, a splash
- ❖ Feta cheese (Danish if possible), a handful
- ❖ Parsley, a handful

Chop the tomatoes, parsley and onions roughly. Mix in a bowl and add the lemon juice, balsamic and crumbled feta.

Serve heaped onto the two slices of toasted bread.

Baked Cauliflower
**

- ❖ Whole cauliflower
- ❖ Breadcrumbs, ½ cup
- ❖ Parmesan, ½ cup
- ❖ Garlic, minced, 1 teaspoon
- ❖ Butter or butter substitute, softened or room temperature, 2 generous dessert spoons

Slice about 2cm off the bottom off the cauliflower head so that it will sit flat. Use a steamer such as the one in the picture on page 18 to steam the cauliflower for about 20 minutes. Test with a skewer to ensure it is soft throughout.

While steaming, combine the butter with the breadcrumbs, parmesan and garlic.

Place the cauliflower in a baking dish and evenly coat the top with the breadcrumb mixture.

Bake at 180 degrees for about 15 minutes or until the crumb is browned.

Note: If you don't own a steamer, you can microwave the cauliflower in a plate or bowl with a bit of water until it is soft. If you don't own a microwave, bake it in the oven first for about 30 minutes or until soft, before adding the breadcrumb coating and baking again.

Baked Creamy Cauliflower
**

- ❖ Whole cauliflower
- ❖ Olive oil, about 2 tablespoons
- ❖ Sour cream, ½ cup
- ❖ Milk, 2 tablespoons

- ❖ Dijon mustard, 1 teaspoon
- ❖ Garlic, minced, 1 teaspoon
- ❖ Cheese, any kind, grated, 1 cup
- ❖ Bacon bits, handful (optional)

Chop the cauliflower into florets (about 3-6cm pieces). Place in a flat baking dish and sprinkle with olive oil, mix to coat. Bake at 200 degrees for about 20 minutes, until the cauliflower is starting to brown at the edges. Remove from oven.

Meanwhile mix together the sour cream, milk, mustard, garlic and half a cup of cheese.

Add the cooked cauliflower to the cream mixture, combine well and return it to the baking dish. Top with the other half cup of cheese. Sprinkle with bacon bits if using. Bake for another 10-15 minutes at 200 degrees or until cheese has melted and beginning to brown.

Brussel Sprouts
*

- ❖ Brussel sprouts, baby or regular
- ❖ Balsamic vinegar
- ❖ Maple Syrup (optional)
- ❖ Olive or vegetable oil
- ❖ Raw plain nuts – walnuts, hazelnuts, almonds – whatever your favourite

Slice off any brown roots from the Brussel sprouts. Cut larger sprouts in half. Arrange in a layer on a baking tray.

Chop the nuts roughly (or crush in another way such as covering with a tea towel and breaking them up with a mallet). Sprinkle the sprouts with the nuts.

Drizzle with oil, maple and balsamic. Bake in the oven at 180 degrees until the sprouts are soft when tested with a skewer (about 30-40 minutes).

Miso Eggplant
**

There are some lesser used ingredients in this, but they will last in the cupboard or fridge (i.e. the white miso) for a long time. You will find other uses for the miso.

❖ Large Eggplant, 2
❖ Vegetable oil, about 2 tablespoons
❖ Sesame seeds, 2 teaspoons

For the sauce:

- ❖ White Miso, 120g
- ❖ Mirin, 100ml
- ❖ Sake, 50ml
- ❖ Sugar, 2 teaspoons

Slice the eggplant lengthways and cut a few slices into the flesh in a criss-cross pattern, without going all the way through to the skin.

Pour a splash of olive oil on the eggplant flesh, spreading it over the flesh with the back of a spoon.

Bake, flesh side up, at about 180 degrees until the eggplant is soft (about 30-40 minutes).

Meanwhile, mix the sauce ingredients until smooth. When the eggplant is soft, take it out of the oven and spread the sauce with a spoon to cover the flesh. Bake for another 15 minutes or until the eggplant is very soft (use a skewer to make sure the middle of the eggplant is cooked through).

Sprinkle with sesame seeds to serve.

Zucchini and Haloumi Stack
*

- ❖ Zucchini
- ❖ Haloumi

Cut zucchini into thin rounds or thin lengthwise strips. Slice haloumi into pieces about 5mm thick. Fry both in a small amount of olive oil until lightly charred. Stack them alternating into piles.

Caramelised Onion
**

- ❖ Onion
- ❖ Olive oil
- ❖ Purple Cabbage (optional)
- ❖ Balsamic Vinegar (*any kind, including fancy ones flavoured with figs, etc*).

Slice onion into rings or half rings and if using, chop purple cabbage into similar sized strips. Pan fry in a little olive oil until beginning to brown. Splash a generous amount of balsamic vinegar into the pan (about a tablespoon for each onion and similar portion of purple cabbage). Fry for a couple more minutes until onion is browned.

Although this is tasty enough to eat on its own, it goes well with a sausage in a roll; a steak sandwich; mixed into rice or pasta; or as an addition to a Club Sandwich (page 70) or Deli Dinner (page 66).

Corn and Cottage Cheese
*

- ❖ Tin of corn kernels (approx. 400g)
- ❖ Container of cottage cheese (approx. 250-350g)
- ❖ Pepper

Combine a tin of well-drained corn kernels with a tub of cottage cheese. Sprinkle with pepper and mix well. This is surprisingly delicious as a side dish or on sandwiches.

Corn Fritters
**

- ❖ Tin of corn kernels (approx. 400g), drained well
- ❖ 2 raw eggs
- ❖ About ¾ cup of flour
- ❖ About ¾ cup of milk or milk substitute
- ❖ Vegetable or olive oil

Optional:

- ❖ Flat bread
- ❖ Mayonnaise
- ❖ Lettuce or baby spinach

In a mixing bowl, stir corn kernels with 2 eggs. Add flour gradually a few spoons at a time until the mixture is thick like a dough. Start adding the milk bit by bit, mixing well.

When the mixture is like a pancake batter (thick but runny enough to drip off the spoon), heat up a splash of oil in a large frypan. When it's bubbling slightly, add spoon-sized dollops of the pancake mixture in batches, so they stay separate. Fry each side for a few minutes or until they are browned on each side.

Optional:

Spread some flat bread with mayonnaise, then wrap a couple of the fritters with some salad leaves. You can eat as is or use a sandwich press to toast the wrap (this works well for the leftovers).

Mashed Potato
*

❖ 1 large potato per person

- ❖ Milk, any kind
- ❖ Butter or butter substitute, 1 dessert spoon
- ❖ Mustard, 1 teaspoon (optional)

Wash and chop potatoes into 3-5cm pieces. Don't bother peeling – as well as being a waste of time, the skin is nutritious. Steam in a saucepan steamer until soft, which should take less than 10 minutes. Mash with a potato masher in the bottom saucepan after you've tipped the boiling water out. Splash in a bit of milk, the mustard if desired and the butter. Keep mashing until smooth.

Roast Potato, Sweet Potato, Pumpkin, Onion *

- ❖ Any kind of potato
- ❖ Sweet potato – orange or especially purple
- ❖ Pumpkin half
- ❖ Onions

Leave the skins on the potatoes - it is edible. Pumpkin skin and onion skin can be left on to roast but will easily peel away once cooked.

So easy it almost doesn't need instruction, but always delicious. Simply roast whole if you have the time (allow at least 90 minutes if you are using large potatoes or a half pumpkin). Test with a skewer to see if it is soft all the way through.

I prefer to chop into smaller pieces, about 3-5cm. For onions, chop into halves or quarters but leave the skins  on and the root attached to keep the onions together. Place in a single layer in a baking tray and splash with olive oil; toss a little to coat as much as possible. Allow 45 minutes to roast at 180 degrees until soft all the way through and starting to brown.

Creamed Spinach
❋❋

- ❖ Bunch fresh Spinach (or box of frozen)
- ❖ Cream, 30ml
- ❖ Pinch of nutmeg
- ❖ Pinch of salt and pepper

Note: a bunch of spinach looks like a lot of spinach, but it reduces to less than 10% of its size when cooked. It's like the disappearing vegetable. This is why it's just as well to use frozen; you know how much you'll have at the end.

Defrost frozen spinach in a colander or just heat it gently in a saucepan. Drain well.

Make sure fresh spinach is thoroughly washed – spinach contains a lot of dirt. Tear the leaves in half. Boil a large saucepan of water and dip the spinach using tongs for about 10 seconds until wilted (you may have to do this in batches). Then dip the spinach into a bowl of cold water to stop it from continuing to cook. Drain and squeeze out water.

Heat the cream, nutmeg and salt/pepper in the hot saucepan (after tipping the water out). Add the spinach and stir to heat through and combine.

Noodles with Vegetables
**

- ❖ Packet of plain soft Asian noodles, not dried. Eg. Udon, Ramen, Soba, Wonton
- ❖ Soy sauce
- ❖ Vegetable oil
- ❖ Minced garlic (from a jar is easiest)
- ❖ Vegetables, roughly chopped, about 3-4 different kinds, eg.:

    - Broccoli
    - Onion
    - Green beans
    - Cauliflower

- Capsicum
- Carrot
- Mushrooms
- Zucchini
- Purple cabbage
- Brussels sprouts
- Fennel

Heat a large saucepan of water until simmering.

Heat a splash of vegetable oil in a frypan. When the pan is hot, add in the chopped vegetables and stir occasionally until cooked, about 5 minutes.

Add the noodles into the simmering water and stir gently. After 5 minutes, strain through a colander.

Add a couple of good splashes of soy and a teaspoon of garlic into the saucepan while it's still hot. Stir to mix, then add back the noodles and mix gently until the noodles are coated in soy sauce.

Add the noodles to the vegetables and mix gently. Serve in bowls.

EGGS

Omelette
* *

- ❖ Eggs – 2 per person
- ❖ Milk - a splash or two
- ❖ Olive or vegetable oil or butter – teaspoon or two

Optional:

- ❖ Grated cheese
- ❖ Haloumi, small pieces
- ❖ Feta, crumbled
- ❖ Baby tomatoes
- ❖ Baby spinach
- ❖ Salami, prosciutto, ham, chicken

Mix the raw eggs and milk very thoroughly with a fork until it's frothy.

If you are using, add the grated cheese or haloumi.

Heat a small frypan to a moderate temperature, about middle of the heat range. Coat the entire surface with a splash of olive oil, or add a spoon of butter and melt it to cover the base so the omelette won't stick anywhere.

Pour in enough egg mixture to reach the edges of the frypan and cook gently for a few minutes. When the underside is lightly browned and the top has mostly set, flip it over for a few more minutes.

To serve, top with one or all of the feta, salami, prosciutto, ham or chicken, spinach, and baby tomatoes.

TOFU

With tofu, it's all about the sauce. Like other bland foods, it's perfect with a delicious sauce as well as being very nutritious. These recipes might change how you feel about tofu.

Sesame Soy Tofu
✳✳✳

- Block of tofu – firm or extra firm approx. 300g
- Sesame oil, about 2 tablespoons
- Sesame seeds, optional

- Vegetable oil, if frying (see below)

For the sauce:

- Soy sauce, ¼ cup
- Garlic, 1 teaspoon
- Brown sugar, 1 teaspoon
- Rice vinegar, ¼ cup
- Cornstarch, 1 tablespoon
- Water, 1 tablespoon
- Sesame oil, ½ tablespoon

Tofu should be a dry as possible. Rinse it under cold water, then dry gently with paper towels or a clean tea towel if you prefer.

Slice the tofu into cubes about 3-4cm in size. Spread out and sprinkle with sesame oil.

Make sauce: mix the cornflour with the water to make a paste. Mix all other ingredients well, except the sesame oil, with the paste.

Either:

1. Oven Bake	2. Fry
Place tofu on a baking tray in a single layer and bake at 180 degrees until golden (about 25 minutes).	Heat a few tablespoons of vegetable oil in a pan and cover the bottom.
Heat the sauce in a saucepan to a simmer until thickened (about 15 minutes). Turn off heat. Add the sesame oil, stir well.	Add the tofu in a single layer and cook each side of each piece for several minutes until golden.
	Add the sauce to the pan and cook with the tofu for a few minutes.
Serve tofu when baked, with the sauce poured over.	Turn off heat and stir in the sesame oil.

Serve with sesame seeds sprinkled on top (optional).

You can serve on its own, with rice, couscous or simple steamed or roasted vegetables.

Peanut Tofu
✳ ✳ ✳

- ❖ Block of tofu – firm or extra firm approx. 300g
- ❖ Sesame oil, about 2 tablespoons

- ❖ Vegetable oil, if frying (see below)

For the sauce:

- ❖ Peanut Butter, ¼ cup
- ❖ Coconut milk, ½ cup (full fat or low fat. You can use other milk if you need to, such as almond or soy. It won't be as creamy but will work).
- ❖ Soy Sauce, 1 tablespoon
- ❖ Brown sugar, 1 tablespoon (or maple/agave syrup)
- ❖ Ginger, grated 1 teaspoon
- ❖ Garlic, grated 1 teaspoon
- ❖ Lime juice, from 1 lime

Tofu should be a dry as possible. Rinse it under cold water, then dry gently with paper towels or a clean tea towel if you prefer.

Slice the tofu into cubes about 3-4cm in size. Spread out and sprinkle with the sesame oil.

Either:

1. Oven Bake	2. Fry
Place on a baking tray in a single layer and bake at 180 degrees until they are golden (about 25 minutes). Heat the sauce in a saucepan to a simmer until thickened (5-10 minutes). Serve cooked tofu with the sauce poured over.	Heat a few tablespoons of vegetable oil in a pan and cover the bottom. Add the tofu in a single layer and cook each side of each piece for several minutes until golden. Add the sauce to the pan and cook with the tofu for a few minutes.

You can serve on its own, with rice, couscous or simple steamed or roasted vegetables.

CHICKEN

Precooked Chicken
*

Pre-cooked hot chicken from a takeaway store or supermarket is versatile and good value. Why cook it yourself when you can get it ready to eat, stuffed and in all different flavours, sometimes for less than the price of a raw chicken? Here are some ways with a hot chicken.

- If you and your fellow diners don't demolish the whole thing in one sitting, chop all the remaining meat off the bones and don't forget to keep the stuffing too, if any.
- Store some of the meat in the fridge for the next day or two.
- Put the rest in ziplock freezer bags and freeze it.
- Throw all the bones into a slow cooker or large pot on the stove. Add enough water to cover; then, if you have them, add some bits of vegetables and herbs you have lying about – parsley, carrots, onion, celery – it's ok if they're a bit past their prime. Use up stalks and leaves. Simmer for a few hours, or for about three hours in the slow cooker on low. Strain the liquid only into takeaway containers (it's useful if they are about a cup each in volume) and label them. Freeze for future use. Throw away the bones and other cooked pieces.
- Use up the fridge pieces: make sandwiches, soups or pasta.
- Use the freezer pieces in the next six months or so.

Honey Soy Chicken
✳✳

You can use any chicken pieces for this - wings, drumstick, thigh - but I suggest not using the breast because it becomes dry when overcooked and doesn't have nearly as much flavour as other parts of the chicken (that's why it's the healthiest - it's the leanest). Cooking the chicken with the bone in is also best, because it keeps the chicken moist and prevents it from shrinking too much.

- Chicken pieces, about 8, with bone
- Honey, quarter of a cup
- Soy Sauce, half a cup
- Garlic, chopped, about a teaspoon, optional
- Ginger, chopped, about a teaspoon, optional
- Sesame seeds, optional

Mix the honey, soy, garlic and ginger in a bowl or tray. Add chicken pieces and cover them with the mixture. Cover with lid or plastic wrap and marinate for 2 hours.

Spread chicken evenly in one layer with the marinade in the same tray (or new one if marinated in a bowl) and sprinkle with a handful of sesame seeds. Bake at 180 degrees for 35 - 40 minutes. Be sure to check that it is cooked right to the bone. There should be no red or dark pink bits near the bone, it should be white.

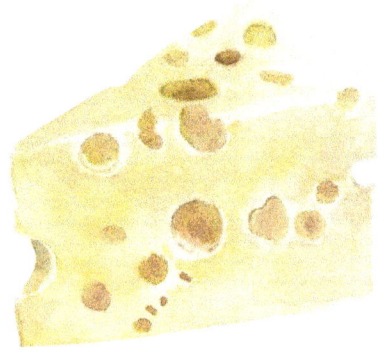

SOUPS

The best thing about a soup is that you can literally chuck various ingredients in the saucepan, boil and eat.

Chicken Soup
**

Chicken soup is not an exact science. You just throw it together and eat it when the vegetables are soft, raw chicken is cooked thoroughly and lentils or peas are completely mushy. I never watch the clock with it, nor do I measure anything - I just throw handfuls in. If you make too much, it is even better the next day, especially if you add pasta.

- Chicken pieces, raw or cooked, preferably with the bone eg. drumsticks or thighs, 1 per person **or** shredded pieces of cooked chicken; whatever you have on hand
- Stock, half a litre per person (you can use water, but it will be nicer with stock)
- Vegetables - onion, carrots, onions, celery, potato, peas, parsnip, cauliflower etc. Frozen is fine

Optional, add any or all:

- Dried pulses - green peas, lentils
- Barley or buckwheat
- Tinned beans - kidney, lima, cannellini etc.

- ❖ Pasta (elbows or small shapes are good)
- ❖ Bacon, chopped into little pieces

Use a large saucepan.

- ✓ If you are using dried peas or lentils, simmer these in the stock for about an hour before adding anything else. Skim away any froth.
- ✓ If you are using raw chicken, add it to the lentils/peas after an hour, or cook it by simmering in the stock until it is white all the way through (about 30-45 minutes depending on size of the chicken pieces).
- ✓ Chop hard vegetables into 2-3cm chunks, removing onion skins but including potato skins. Add to the pot. They will take about 30 minutes to soften.
- ✓ Add pasta, green vegetables and cooked chicken pieces to the pot about 20 minutes before serving.

Tip: Avoid dried beans such as kidney beans and lima beans. They are toxic unless they are cooked for a long time at boiling temperature. Tinned beans are easiest.

Pea and Ham Soup

*

**

This recipe will make a lot of soup (for at least 4) but it freezes well for later.

- Ham or bacon bones, smoked – one large or several smaller ones. The more meat on them, the better.
- Green dried split peas, one bag
- Stock, about 2 litres or more, enough to cover the ham bones

Optional:

- Onion, chopped roughly
- Carrot, celery, potato, other root vegetables, chopped roughly
- Frozen peas
- Bacon or ham pieces, pre-cooked (packet ham or smoked bacon is perfect)

Add the stock, dried peas and ham hock into a large saucepan and simmer for between 1½ - 2 hours, until the meat is falling off the bones and the peas are soft. You can stir it occasionally.

About 30 minutes before serving, add in frozen peas and bacon or ham pieces.

Chicken and Corn Soup
*

❖ Creamed corn, 1 can
❖ Cooked chicken pieces
❖ Egg, 1
❖ Soy sauce, splash of

Warm the tin of creamed corn in a saucepan. Add the chicken pieces and the soy sauce. Beat the egg with a fork in a small bowl until the egg is combined, then stir through the soup. Serve hot, with buttered toast if desired.

MEATBALLS

Minced meat – beef, lamb, chicken, pork – whatever you choose – makes terrific meatballs. You can make a stack of these and save some for tomorrow, freeze them raw or cook them and then freeze them.

I discovered a cheat way to make mini meatballs when I can't be bothered to roll them: use a silicon muffin tray. You can spoon the meat in, press it down and they're ready for the oven.

Meatballs
✳✳✳

❖ Minced meat, about 600g
❖ Egg, 1
❖ Milk, splash of

Options, add one or some of these (but especially add a sauce, and a vegetable if you can):

- Breadcrumbs, about half a cup
- Onion, finely chopped
- Minced garlic, teaspoon
- Worcestershire sauce, good splash of
- Tomato Sauce, 2 tablespoons; OR Tomato Paste, 2 tablespoons

- Grated Carrot
- Spinach, finely chopped
- Zucchini, finely chopped

Mix all ingredients together well and either shape into golf balls or use a silicon muffin pan. If you've made golf balls, arrange on a tray in one layer.

Bake at 180 degrees for about 20 minutes, or until brown.

Serve with:

- Pasta, any kind
- Polenta
- Rice or other grain
- Mashed potato
- Any vegetable
- Soy sauce (optional)

Mini Muffin Meatballs; to avoid the bother of rolling perfectly even balls.

Served here with plain fettucine. Even my child eats this, she doesn't seem to notice the zucchini in them.

Meatball in a Roll
*

Use up any leftover meatballs by putting them in a fresh bread roll with a bit of sauce (tomato, BBQ, mayonnaise, chilli, etc). Heat them in the microwave first, and if you have them, add some other bits and pieces like pickled cucumbers, beetroot, baby spinach, tomato, onion, avocado or red cabbage.

PRE-MADE SUPERMARKET MEALS

You don't have to feel guilty about using partly prepared meals - not all of them are high in salt, fat or sugar. Here are some products you can find that are packaged and ready to cook, some frozen and some fresh. Some will be somewhat high in salt, so take care to check the salt content and eat in moderation. The maximum salt intake per day is 2000mg for an adult, which is about a teaspoon. Children should be eating less than half of this depending on their age, and note that these guidelines are maximums; we should try to eat less than this. If you are eating something salty, pair it with plain vegetables if possible.

Marinated Steaks in Vacuum Sealed Packs
*

Supermarkets sell all kinds of meat in vacuum sealed packs, which last much longer than in regular packaging and can be seasoned or marinated. Marinated meat is more tender and has more flavour than plain meat.

Marinated steak can be fried on both sides (no need for oil, the marinade will provide the moisture) until it is done to your liking. Let it rest on a chopping board for a couple of minutes, so the juices don't run out as much when it is sliced. Serve as is, or slice and serve with other recipes in this book (couscous, vegetables, potato mash or in a sandwich or wrap).

Fresh Fish
*

Buy fish in fillets, sliced and deboned. Leave the skin on when cooking, as it will come off more easily after cooking if you don't want to eat it. My general rule is: the more expensive the fish, the better it tastes (salmon is one of my favourites).

Fish is very quick to fry – just a few minutes on each side in a little oil depending on the size of the fish. It should be lightly brown on the outside and only just cooked in the middle. Cooked fish will fall apart easily, raw fish won't.

Alternatively, put it in an oven on a tray at 180 degrees for about 10 minutes (again, depending on the size of the fish – check the middle before serving).

You can also microwave fish. It should only take a few minutes – check regularly.

Serve with a lemon wedge with recipes in this book – for example couscous, rice, or a vegetable salad.

Frozen Fish, Scallops or Prawns
*

Great to have in the freezer, you can buy frozen seafood that is ready to tip into a frypan, frozen, and gently fry until cooked through. You can serve it with lemon wedges, or this sauce.

Lemon Butter Sauce
*

- ❖ Butter, about 2 heaped spoons
- ❖ Garlic, minced, 1-2 teaspoons
- ❖ Lemon juice from 1 lemon
- ❖ Spoonful of fresh parsley, chopped (optional)

Melt the butter gently in a small saucepan on a low heat. After a few minutes, add in the rest of the ingredients and mix. The sauce should be slightly browned. Serve warm.

Dumplings (Yum Cha style)
**

These are high in salt so try not to live on them. These are my two favourite ways to cook them.

- For pork and vegetable dumplings: Boil in a saucepan of gently boiling water until they are soft and floating on the surface of the water. Remove with tongs, shake off the water. Heat a frypan with a splash of oil and fry the dumplings, turning until they are lightly brown on all sides.

- For prawn dumplings: put in a steamer saucepan that's been lightly sprayed or wiped with olive oil. Steam for about 10 minutes, or until the dumplings have become almost translucent.

Try throwing a couple of handfuls of frozen peas into the steamer or frypan a minute before serving.

Hot Smoked Salmon in Vacuum Sealed Packs
**

This is already cooked, so you can throw it easily into cooked rice, pasta, or couscous (note, you can make this recipe with tinned fish of any kind).

- ❖ Packet of hot smoked salmon
- ❖ Pasta - any kind
- ❖ Sour Cream - about 300ml
- ❖ Green vegetable - broccoli, zucchini, peas
- ❖ Mustard, about 2 teaspoons (optional)

Make the pasta according to packet instructions and according to how many people you are cooking for. This is often difficult to determine given that pasta increases in size when it's cooked, but here is a rough guide:

- A cup per person for small pasta
- For larger pasta, about a cup and a half per person
- A bunch of long pasta about the thickness of a bottle cap for two people

Meanwhile, lightly fry up some chopped vegetables in a saucepan. Usually, I go for a green vegetable, but you can use anything you like. After 5 minutes, add in the sour cream and mustard, mix, and then add the salmon, breaking it up into small pieces.

When the pasta is done, drain it, add it back to the pan with the vegetables and mix it together.

Burritos and Tacos
**

- ❖ Taco or Burrito Kit
- ❖ Minced meat, about 600g
- ❖ Tomatoes
- ❖ Avocado
- ❖ Sour Cream

Follow pack instructions, which basically entails frying the meat, adding the meat flavouring and a little water so it isn't too dry, and mixing it through properly over heat for 10 minutes.

These kits contain a meat flavouring which is high in salt, so it is best eaten with a selection of vegetables. I like to use ones that don't require cooking.

Tip: Any leftover meat can be used in the leftover tacos or burritos using a sandwich press.

PASTA

Possibly the most commonly made pasta dish is "spag bol" – so in the quest for originality, I won't put it here. Here are some non-spaghetti bolognaise recipes instead.

Creamy Pasta with Greens
✳✳✳

Serving size is for about 2, but any leftovers will be good for the following day or two.

- A cup per person for small pasta
- For larger pasta, about a cup and a half per person
- A bunch of long pasta about the diameter of a bottle cap for two people

❖ Spaghetti, fettucine, or any pasta of your choice
❖ Splash of oil (vegetable, olive, any other cooking oil)
❖ Zucchini, broccoli, beans of peas (frozen are fine)
❖ Sour cream, about 200ml
❖ Mustard, 1-2 teaspoons

Optional:

❖ Ham, sliced into small pieces
❖ Bacon, sliced into small pieces

Cook the pasta according to packet directions (or just boil in a saucepan until it's just soft, between 8-15 minutes depending on the pasta). Do not overcook or it will be soggy. Drain pasta in a colander.

Chop any larger vegetables into bite size pieces. Heat the oil in a frypan and add any uncooked meat (e.g., bacon) and fry until lightly brown. Add vegetables and cook for 5 minutes until slightly soft (longer if you prefer).

Stir in sour cream and mustard. Add cooked pasta and stir through for a few minutes until hot and well mixed.

PUFF PASTRY PIZZA
**

Totally, utterly cheating but surprisingly good.

❖ Puff pastry, one sheet for two people

Any of the following: use a handful each of these 3-5 ingredients:

❖ Caramelised onion (see under Vegetables) – this is the only item I pre-cook, because I don't like half cooked onion. Feel free to slice it thinly and throw it on without cooking first, if you don't mind crunchy onion.
❖ Sliced mushroom
❖ Sundried or semi-sundried tomatoes
❖ Spinach, broccoli
❖ Baby corn
❖ Corn kernels
❖ Peas
❖ Any other small bits of vegetable
❖ Sliced cooked meat of any kind, in small pieces
❖ Haloumi or feta, in small pieces
❖ Optional: pizza sauce – tomato, barbecue, or chutney

Preheat the oven to moderate (about 180 degrees).

Let the puff pastry defrost; this will take about 10 minutes. Lay it onto a large oven tray with baking paper underneath, or a light spray of oil.

Spread a little sauce, if using, on the puff pastry.

Layer the chosen ingredients evenly on top.

Bake for about 15 minutes, until you can see the edges of the pastry puff up and start to brown.

CURRIES
✳✳✳

It's so easy to eat lots of vegetables when they are cooked with coconut milk and some sort of curry paste. It's much more interesting than a plain stir fry.

This recipe will make enough for four hungry people, or two with leftovers for tomorrow.

You will note that this is a vegetarian curry, but you can add your choice of meat at the onion stage - just brown it with the onions and continue with vegetables.

- ❖ Jar of some kind of curry – Indian, Asian – the choice is yours

About three of the following:

- ❖ Potato – about four small or equivalent
- ❖ Sweet potato - small

- ❖ Pumpkin – medium cut slice
- ❖ Eggplant
- ❖ Mushroom – a few handfuls
- ❖ Green Beans – a few handfuls
- ❖ Cauliflower – a quarter to a half
- ❖ Onion – one large
- ❖ Capsicum - one

Also include:

- ❖ Dash of olive oil
- ❖ Tin of coconut milk 400 ml (or coconut cream if you want to be decadent)
- ❖ Cup of stock – 250ml vegetable or chicken
- ❖ Rice or couscous

Optional:

- ❖ Banana
- ❖ Sultanas

Slice onions roughly. Chop the other vegetables into chunks – about the size of a large mouthful.

Use a large saucepan or pot.

Fry up the onion in the oil first for a few minutes until they brown a little. Throw in your other vegetables and cook for a few more minutes.

Add about 2 tablespoons of the curry paste and mix.

Add the stock and coconut milk/cream.

Simmer for about 20-30 minutes with no lid. The sauce needs to be thick and any potatoes soft.

Add in sliced banana and a handful of sultanas, if using. Stir through.

Serve with rice or couscous, or eat on its own if you can't be bothered.

DELI DINNERS
**

It's called a deli dinner because it's mostly food items you can buy from the deli section of the supermarket. This is the ultimate in lazy food preparation, because it's just a selection of delicious things with minimum cooking. My family is crazy about deli dinners – I should just serve them every night. Choose from the following ingredients and put 5 or more on each plate (try to include a couple of vegetables). Dinner is done.

- Prosciutto, salami, other cured meats
- Cold ham, chicken, beef slices
- Smoked salmon, trout
- Rollmops
- Pickled cucumbers
- Pickled onions
- Boiled egg
- Cheese: brie, camembert, cheddar, Babybel, anything you like

- Mushroom (raw)
- Broccoli (raw)
- Carrot (raw)
- Capsicum (raw)
- Celery (raw, of course)
- Edamame (microwave frozen beans in a splash of water for a minute or so, until hot)
- Baby tomatoes
- Avocado
- Apple
- Anything else you think would be complimentary

Tip: if you're trying to feed small fussy children, they may eat raw vegetables if you cut them into shapes. Try a crimped knife or cutting them into tiny cubes or batons.

This $2 knife gets my daughter eating "carrot chips" It also makes fancy sliced potato for baking.

Tip: get an egg cooker from a variety store. They are inexpensive and will cook 1 to 6 eggs perfectly every time with no guesswork.

Here's one of our Deli Dinners. It's not even close to Masterchef - but every single bit gets eaten, even by the fussy child. We had this with a warm bowl of couscous on the side.

SANDWICHES

Sandwiches make perfectly good dinners. You don't have to confine them to lunches. You can use a sandwich press to toast them when the bread that isn't particularly fresh.

You can also use any kind of wrap for these combinations - e.g., Lebanese bread, leftover burritos, or any flat bread. Toast in the sandwich press if preferred.

Sandwich Suggestions
*

**

I haven't listed measurements on here because for the most part, they don't really matter - sandwiches can be about using up stuff in the fridge or freezer to make something filling enough that fits inside two pieces of bread.

Tip: when you are mixing with mayonnaise, add it gradually so you don't use too much, as mayonnaise is quite rich. As a guide, use a third the volume of your other filling (e.g., a cup of chicken to a third of a cup of mayonnaise).

Tip: when adding lemon juice, be sparing as it is a strong flavour and can make fillings too runny. You only need about a squeeze per sandwich.

Try:

- Leftover hot chicken, mayonnaise, cucumber
- Chicken or any other cold meat, avocado
- Baked beans
- Grated carrot, cream cheese, sultanas and sprouts (trust me, it's good)
- Banana, peanut butter
- Banana, tahini
- Egg, mayonnaise (mix together)
- Egg, mayonnaise mixed with a teaspoon of curry powder (mix together)
- Bacon, avocado, mayonnaise, tomato
- Prawns (defrosted mini frozen), mayonnaise, lemon juice, dill (mix ingredients together)
- Tinned tuna in springwater (well drained), mayonnaise, coriander, chili (mix together)
- Tinned corn, cottage cheese
- Cream cheese, banana, honey (if your child is fussy, at least this will give them some fruit)

If you are up to it, make a

Club Sandwich
✽✽✽

This will take between 15-30 minute to assemble depending on how many ingredients you add.

Start with a base of:

❖ Toasted bread, 2 slices per sandwich
❖ Mayonnaise, BBQ or tomato sauce

Then add a few of the following:

- Cooked meat: e.g., bacon, prosciutto, ham, steak or chicken
- Fried egg
- Baby spinach (raw or quickly fried) or any lettuce, shredded
- Mushrooms (raw or cooked)
- Sliced tomato
- Grated carrot
- Pickled cucumber, sliced
- Plain cucumber, sliced
- Cheese (cheddar, haloumi, feta, or any sliced)
- Onion (caramelized, see page 27 or simply fry slices in a little oil or butter until brown)

I added some leftover sliced steak to this Club Sandwich - I never make the same sandwich twice but they're always delicious.

I wonder if chocolate thinks about me too

SAUCES

Salad Dressing with Miso
*

- Any oil, ¼ cup
- Any Vinegar, ¼ cup
- White Miso, tablespoon
- Sesame Oil, a splash
- Maple Syrup, a splash
- Soy Sauce, a splash

Mix together well.

Peanut Dressing for Meat or Tofu
*

- Peanut Butter or other nut butter, ½ cup
- Rice Vinegar, ¼ cup
- Soy Sauce or tamari, ¼ cup
- Honey, 3 spoons
- Ginger, grated, 1 teaspoon
- Garlic, grated, 1 teaspoon

Mix together thoroughly.

Sauce for Fish

*

- ❖ Butter, about 2 heaped spoons
- ❖ Garlic, minced, 1-2 teaspoons
- ❖ Lemon juice from 1 lemon
- ❖ Spoonful of fresh parsley, chopped (optional)

Melt the butter gently in a small saucepan on a low heat. After a few minutes, add in the rest of the ingredients and mix. The sauce should be slightly browned. Serve warm.

DESSERTS

If you want a hot dessert that requires not too much cooking or at least very easy preparation, here are some options.

French Toast
**

- ❖ Bread (better if a little stale, it will hold together more easily)
- ❖ Egg (1 egg per two slices of bread)
- ❖ Honey, Maple Syrup, Rice Syrup or other syrup
- ❖ Fruit (optional)

Warm up a small frypan and melt a teaspoon of butter or butter substitute. Cover the bottom of the pan with the melted butter as far as possible.

Crack an egg into a small plastic plate with a lip or Tupperware container about the size of a piece of bread. Whisk it with a fork until the yolk and white are completely mixed. Place a piece of bread into the egg, both sides, for a few seconds until the bread is soaked. Cook both sides in the pan (a spatula is best for flipping). The toast should be nicely browned (1-2 minutes on each side). Serve with a syrup and/or fruit.

Tapioca
✳✳✳

Instructions for making tapioca will be on the box, but this is my favourite way of making it.

- ❖ Tapioca pearls, ½ a cup
- ❖ Water, 600ml
- ❖ Any milk or coconut cream, about 150ml
- ❖ Fruit – banana, strawberries, raspberries, etc
- ❖ Syrup – honey, golden, maple, rice malt, etc

Boil the water in a saucepan and add the tapioca pearls. Start stirring gently and continue for about 15-20 minutes. The tapioca will expand and thicken and become completely transparent. *You must stir continually until this happens, otherwise it will burn on the bottom.*

When transparent, turn the heat off, put the lid on and leave for 10-15 minutes.

Add milk/coconut milk, stir it through (you may quickly reheat at this stage). Serve warm with fruit and a spoon of syrup.

This can be refrigerated and later served cold.

Bread and Butter Pudding
✳ ✳ ✳

- ❖ Bread, any sort including wholemeal (at least 6 slices, better if a little stale)
- ❖ Butter, enough for spreading on each slice
- ❖ Jam, enough for spreading on each slice
- ❖ Sultanas, or other chopped dried fruit – a couple of handfuls
- ❖ Egg – one egg per 4 slices of bread
- ❖ Milk – any kind
- ❖ Sugar (optional) – 1 teaspoon for 4 slices of bread

Lightly butter and jam each piece of bread. You don't have to remove the crusts; they cook perfectly well. Cut the bread slices into 4 triangles and arrange them in a glass or ceramic dish, or aluminium tray.

Leave small gaps between each piece and create 2-3 layers – and *sprinkle the dried fruit between the first and second layers - don't put it on top, it will burn,* with the last layer as decorative as you can make it for wow factor.

Mix up your eggs well with a fork, then add milk and mix well. If you wish to add sugar, you can stir it through. (I find the jam/fruit to be enough of a sweetener, but if it isn't you can always add honey when serving.)

Pour the egg and milk mixture over the bread and press the bread pieces down to make sure they are all well

soaked. If there isn't enough, make more or just top up with a little milk. The bread is very absorbent.

Bake for about an hour at 180 degrees in a bain marie – this is a tray filled with about an inch of water for your pudding pan to sit in while baking, to keep the pudding moist.

The pudding is done when there is no more egg/milk liquid at the bottom of the pan – it should all be absorbed and cooked through. If it isn't, keep baking until it is fully absorbed.

Custard
**

- ❖ Custard Powder, 3 tablespoons
- ❖ Sugar, 1 tablespoon
- ❖ Milk, 2½ cups

Optional:

❖ Banana
❖ Sultanas or currants
❖ Dried/fresh/tinned fruit
❖ Nuts

Add milk to a saucepan and heat until simmering. Slowly pour in the custard, stirring as you add so that it doesn't go lumpy. Continue stirring as it thickens. (If you don't stir continuously, lumps will form – if so, break them up with your spoon).

When smooth, serve with a topping of any of the optional ingredients.

Polenta Porridge
*

This is delicious for dessert or for breakfast. Sometimes I even give it to my daughter for afternoon tea.

❖ Polenta
❖ Milk

Optional:

❖ Banana

- ❖ Sultanas
- ❖ Dried/fresh/tinned fruit
- ❖ Nuts
- ❖ Honey
- ❖ Cream

Use polenta in the ratio of 1:4 polenta:milk. For example:

½ cup polenta, 2 cups milk (for 2 people approx.)
1 cup polenta, 4 cups milk (for 4 people approx.)

Add milk to a saucepan and heat until simmering. Slowly pour in the polenta, stirring as you add so that it doesn't go lumpy. It will thicken very quickly. Add a splash of milk if it's too thick.

Serve with a topping of any of the optional ingredients.

INDEX

Bread and Butter Pudding, 77
Bruschetta, 21
Brussel Sprouts, 24
Burritos and Tacos, 58
Cauliflower, Baked, 22
Cauliflower, Creamy Baked, 23
Chicken, 42
Chicken and Corn Soup, 48
Chicken Soup, 45
Chicken, Honey Soy, 43
Chicken, Precooked, 42
Club Sandwich, 70
Corn and Cottage Cheese, 28
Corn Fritters, 28
Couscous with Egg, 12
Couscous, Basic, 11
Creamy Pasta with Greens, 60
Curries, 64
Custard, 78
Deli Dinners, 66
Desserts, 75
Dumplings (Yum Cha style), 55
Eggplant, Miso, 25

Eggs, 34
Fish, Fresh, 54
Fish, Scallops or Prawns, Frozen, 55
French Toast, 75
Lemon Butter Sauce, 55
Meatball in a Roll, 51
Meatballs, 49
Noodles with Vegetables, 32
Omelette, 34
Onion, Caramelised, 27
Pasta, 60
Pea and Ham Soup, 47
Polenta, Basic, 13
Polenta, Fried, 14
Polenta, Porridge, 79
Potato, Mashed, 29
Puff Pastry Pizza, 63
Raw Vegetable Salad, 19
Rice Pilaf, 15
Rice with Boiled Egg, 16
Sandwich Suggestions, 69
Sandwiches, 69
Sauces, 73
Smoked Salmon - Hot, 57
Soups, 45
Spinach, Creamed, 31

Steaks, Marinated, 53
Tapioca, 76
Tofu, 37
Tofu - Peanut, 39
Tofu – Sesame Soy, 37

Vegetables, 18
Vegetables, Roasted, 30
Zucchini and Haloumi
   Stack, 27

REFERENCES

https://www.heartfoundation.org.au/heart-health-education/salt-and-heart-health

https://minimalistbaker.com/how-to-cook-white-rice/

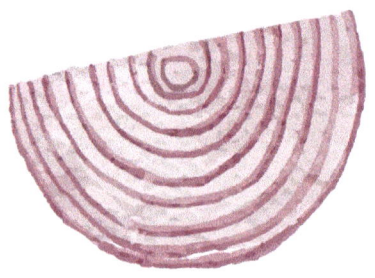

Tonight's Menu: Beggars can't be choosers

www.ingramcontent.com/pod-product-compliance
Lightning Source LLC
Chambersburg PA
CBHW062042290426
44109CB00026B/2707